# MASSACHUSETTS

*Photography by*
ROBERT KAUFMAN

*Text by*
ROBERT HALE

*Captions by*
CHRISTINA TREE

✖ GRAPHIC ARTS CENTER PUBLISHING COMPANY, PORTLAND, OREGON

International Standard Book Number 1-55868-093-6
Library of Congress Number 92-70118
© MCMXCII by Graphic Arts Center Publishing Company
P.O. Box 10306 • Portland, Oregon 97210 • 503/226-2402
All rights reserved.
No part of this book may be reproduced by any means
without written permission of the publisher.
President • Charles M. Hopkins
Editor-in-Chief • Douglas A. Pfeiffer
Managing Editor • Jean Andrews
Designer • Robert Reynolds
Color Separations • Agency Litho
Typographer • Harrison Typesetting
Printer • Rono Graphic Communications Co.
Bindery • Lincoln & Allen
Printed and bound in the United States of America

To my father,
S. David Kaufman

ROBERT KAUFMAN

# MASSACHUSETTS

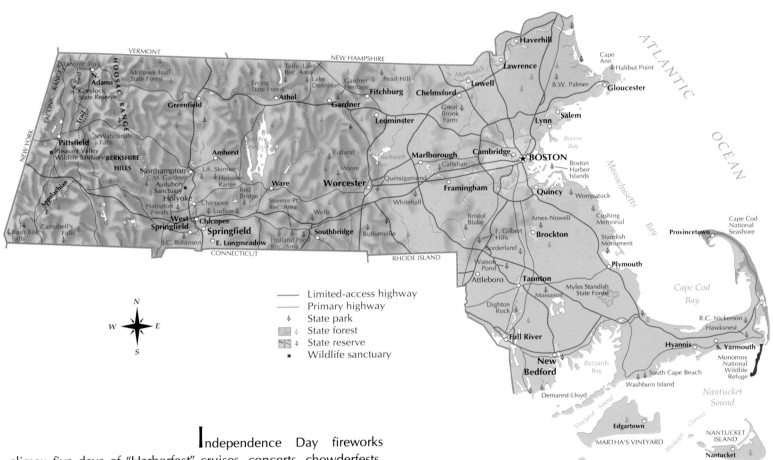

Independence Day fireworks climax five days of "Harborfest" cruises, concerts, chowderfests, reenactments, and parades, more than a hundred events celebrating Boston's incendiary role in the Revolution. ◄ ◄ ◄ Foliage season is a call to the woods. ◄ ◄ The world's oldest commissioned warship afloat, the USS *Constitution* was launched in 1797 and saved from the scrapyard in 1830 when "Old Ironsides," a poem by Harvard student Oliver Wendell Holmes, won her national fame and a Congressional appropriation. She sailed on into the 1930s and now welcomes visitors at the Charlestown Navy Yard. ►

The Appalachian Trail, a hiking path from Georgia to Maine, was proposed by Benton MacKay of Shirley, Massachusetts, in 1921. It threads the Berkshires, traversing the spine of the Mount Greylock Range. ◄ Foliage hues begin in Northern Berkshire and the Hampshire Hilltowns in late September, then spread to the valleys and coastal towns and linger there well into October. ▲ Baseball in Boston is no mere spectator sport, especially on a sunny summer day at Fenway Park, when the Red Sox are winning and everyone in the bleachers is "doing the wave." ► ►

The North Shore's beaches are far more accessible in winter than in summer. No parking lots are jealously guarded, and there is an invitation to quiet release. ▲ A winter snow storm slows rush hour traffic on the Massachusetts Turnpike, muting sound and speed. The state's only toll road, the "Mass Pike" runs 135 miles from Boston to the New York State line, linking the Bay to the Berkshires in just over two hours. ▶

Billed as "the only natural bridge in North America" and "150 million years older than Niagara Falls," the Natural Bridge has been a tourist attraction for more than a century and a half. Its pond and marble dam now form the centerpiece for Natural Bridge State Park, just west of North Adams. ◄ The late afternoon sun invites a pause on Nantucket's exclusive Wauwinet Beach at the narrow, northeastern tip of the island. ▲

The massive, Romanesque-style tower of Trinity Church dominated Copley Square in the late nineteenth century. It has since been dwarfed by Back Bay high rises, shadowed by the sheer glass walls of Boston's highest skyscraper, the sixty-two-story John Hancock Tower. ▲ For much of the year the Charles River is a meeting site for scullers from Harvard, Boston University, Northeastern, and MIT. The Head of the River Regatta draws college and university teams from throughout the East. ► Mill buildings along Newton Upper Falls made silk and silk-making machinery. The Boston suburb also produced the Fig Newton. ► ►

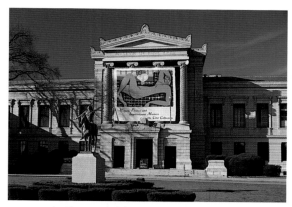

*Boston's Museum of Fine Art*

Geographically, Massachusetts is a small state, but historically, culturally, educationally, and any number of other ways, it is enormous. You can drive across it the long way, from the Atlantic Ocean through the Berkshires to the border of New York State, in three hours. Yet you could spend a lifetime, as some have, studying its impact on the nation of which it became the sixth state, one hundred years after Massachusetts colonists overthrew British Governor Sir Edmund Andros, an early act of rebellion in the long struggle for independence.

The sites of those long-ago struggles are hallowed spots, and the men and women who engaged the enemy are regarded as continuing presences, as are so many foundation figures in our national heritage—the Adams family, John Hancock, Thoreau and Emerson, Longfellow, Hawthorne, Melville, Holmes, and dozens of others who called Massachusetts home.

This sense of living history, of history going on now, is never taken for granted by those born and raised in Massachusetts. Newcomers find it a vastly appealing phenomenon. It is only one reason many of the tens of thousands of young people who come to schools and colleges in the Commonwealth each year from all over the world stay on when their courses are complete. Some of the others are easy accessibility to a great variety of arts and ethnic cultures, major athletics, continuing and vast educational opportunities, the possibility of living in a rural setting, yet being only minutes away from all that a modern city has to offer.

This essay is the impressions of one of those who came to Massachusetts to study, and stayed, who went "home" on schedule but missed the Massachusetts mix, the furious energy that is part of every political and athletic event, performances by international artists, the smell of the sea, the color of the hills, the taste of fresh-from-the-shell fried clams, a "nor'easter's" winds and rain, the magnificent domestic architecture to be found in almost every city and town in the Commonwealth, and that feeling of being in the midst of history ongoing, a feeling that gives one hope for the future as well as pride in the past.

The past is not always the way legend has it. The Pilgrim Separatists thought they were headed for Virginia when nature's force decided otherwise and blew them into Massachusetts Bay, where they disembarked first at what is now Provincetown, and then on Clark's Island in Duxbury Bay. There they celebrated a religious service of thanksgiving before proceeding in toward the mouth of a mainland brook that promised a steady supply of fresh water. An example of history ongoing is that each year—not in December when the Pilgrims stopped there, but in June—a sizeable group of people from Plymouth and Duxbury go by boat out to Clark's Island to picnic and then to hold a service of remembrance by the rock (which is much more impressive than Plymouth Rock) that sheltered the Pilgrim prayers. Each year the story is retold and application to the world of today is made.

Most people picture the tired but hardy band stepping straight off the Mayflower after a long and terrible crossing onto a conveniently placed rock—which is now protected by a parthenon-inspired granite canopy. Whether that rock was truly there (it has been moved several times over the centuries) is open to conjecture. Legend

*Nantucket Square in Nantucket Town*

goes on to have them kneeling and naming this spot Neuw Plimoth after the English port from whence they embarked.

Actually, King Charles had already given New Plymouth its name, which appeared on a coastal map drawn by John Smith half a dozen years prior to the Pilgrims' landing. The king, with no sense of modesty, also named the great river on Smith's map the Charles, and the cape to the north after his mother, Ann. They remain so named.

Thanks to those already living along these shores, about half of the Pilgrims survived that first winter. The tentative, but not completely hostile, locals were Wampanoags. Their neighbors were the Pawtucketts, Nipmucks, and Pokumtakukes. Growers primarily, they continued to gather and hunt as their ancestors had done for thousands of years. The success these tribes had achieved in living peacefully side by side, generally in villages with similar social structures and all speaking an Algonquian dialect, allowed them to be less threatening to the pale and hairy strangers than they might otherwise have been.

Fields that Native Americans had kept fertile through methods handed down generation after generation would shortly grow abundant crops for the Pilgrims, who copied the Wampanoags' practices. They also learned Native ways to harvest shellfish and plentiful game. Stalwart as they were, the lives of these newcomers were literally in the hands of the Americans who preceded them here.

Romantic as it is to believe, the Pilgrims were not even the first Europeans to walk the rocky shore. Earlier visitors go back to Norsemen around the year A.D. 1000, Giovanni da Verrazano in 1524, followed by a spate of explorers in the early 1600s— Bartholomew Gosnold, Martin Pring, Samuel Champlain, George Weymouth, George Popham (who tried to colonize the area which he called Northern Virginia), Henry Hudson, Adriaen Block, and John Smith.

In fact, while they were not greeted on arrival by a Native American speaking English, the Pilgrims had not been long ashore before Samoset appeared in their midst, having walked down from what is now the state of Maine, to engage the newcomers in conversation using their own language, which he had acquired from British fishermen who had been harvesting in the waters off the coast for at least half a century, trading, meanwhile, with those Columbus called Indians.

It is assumption that European explorers discovered this land for mankind, when for several millennia it had been peopled by numerous tribes with their own flourishing civilizations. Most chronologies of Massachusetts history begin with European arrivals, but archaeological sites indicate there were thriving settlements of farming people dating back as far as 6000 to 10,000 B.C. These much earlier people originated in Asia or Asia Minor. A tribe of their descendents called themselves the Massachuset. It was their name that would be given first to the area and then to the Commonwealth. European explorers and then settlers would eventually, first through disease and then warfare, decimate much of those established populations they found here.

None of this takes anything away from the heroic achievements of early European settlers, nor indeed from the waves of immigrants that would follow in ever-increasing numbers over the next three centuries. We talk about development of land today with the attendant loss of open spaces and great shiftings of population, but it has been ever thus since that first successful settlement in Plimoth Plantation in 1620. Within

*Polaroid Corporation Headquarters, Cambridge*

two decades of the Pilgrim landing, twenty-five towns in Massachusetts had been incorporated, stretching from Yarmouth in the middle of Cape Cod; north to Ipswich, Rowley, and Newbury; and west to Concord, Sudbury, and Dedham—all of this in territory that had served Native Americans in very different ways.

The response of the proper Bostonian who, when asked which direction she took on her trip around the world, said "West by way of Dedham" is often repeated to indicate the insularity of Bostonians in the late nineteenth century. In the mid-seventeenth century, individuals from the Massachusetts Bay Colony, of which Boston was a part, and from Plimoth Plantation were anything but insular, moving deep into wilderness to establish isolated communities usually with only one or two families. Occasionally stakes were made and a "town" established by a single intrepid settler.

While these mostly English colonists at first accepted the already given Native American names for rivers and mountains—Assabet, Squannacook, Nobscot, Pisgah—and occasionally followed the Natives' custom of acknowledging nature's bounty by calling places Deerfield, Medway, Longmeadow, Brookfield, they mostly gave their settlements names that reminded them of home—Leicester, Oxford, Dartmouth—or commemorated earlier settlers—Belchertown, Shirley, Dalton, Williamstown.

This random method of naming the 351 cities and towns that exist today leads to marvelous confusions for the visitor who doesn't know the difference between Ashburnham, Ashby, Ashfield, and Ashland; or Eastham, Easthampton, and Easton; to say nothing of Bridgewater, East Bridgewater, and West Bridgewater; or South Hadley, Southampton, Southborough, Southbridge, and Southwick. As a newcomer, I was especially taken with Assinippi and Athol.

There are differences, however, glorious differences. Each town and city has its own flavor, its own special quality, its own sense of self. Much of this has to do with ethnicity, because while Englishmen landed early, they were soon followed by other Europeans and French Canadians, each group bringing its own cultural heritage. For numbers of good reasons they clung to what they brought as they also adapted to that which was already here.

A major reason was simple unfriendliness. Native Americans were no more belli-cose to early Europeans than those Europeans were to later arrivals. The Pilgrims came to practice religion in their own way, not to establish religious freedom for anybody else, which meant they did not suffer those who wanted to worship in any other way. Difference was not tolerated. The Bay Colony Puritans were no more open. Quakers were persecuted and driven from place to place, as were Shakers later, and all other groups or individuals who developed a variation in the accepted expression of faith. Protestants with positions of power early on kept Catholics in controlled corners. While Jews were not forced into ghettos, they did create their own enclaves.

As the first settlers developed into what came to be called Yankees, they established particular ways of doing everything from praying to politics. Those who followed, because of the Yankees' determination not to share power, clung together for mutual support. Forced to live in subcommunities, these people for long periods of time retained their special identities, and in some cases their own language. Centuries later, having long since taken control of their lives and their communities, ethnic groups continue to dominate in parts of the state and in specific towns: Americans of Irish,

*Boston Common*

Italian, Portuguese, Polish, Russian, French Canadian, German descent. And today there are growing populations, especially in the cities, of African Americans, peoples from Spanish-speaking countries, and most recently those of Asian origin. Each group finds itself following the same long path to acceptance and eventual political voice that earlier arrivals trod.

While amalgamation and acquisition of political power has sometimes dulled the edges of ethnic differences, the richness of cultural diversity remains, thanks first to those years of exclusivity and more recently to growing awareness of, and pride in, one's national or racial heritage.

It is sad to note that there is only one small area of Martha's Vineyard where Native Americans continue to make their presence felt. What these people had to contribute was mostly destroyed centuries ago by the usurpers of their land and nation.

Ethnic diversity with the annual festivals that celebrate Albanian, Armenian, Cape Verdean, Greek, Scottish, and every other national origin's traditions is one of the state's most valuable resources. While the descendents of the famous Adams family are meeting in Quincy, and the Alden kindred is gathering in Duxbury, all across the Commonwealth families from Pakistan or Angola, Europe and Asia are coming together to add to the rich stew that replaces what was an old Yankee bastion. This is the present state in Massachusetts.

The Massachusetts economy in the beginning was based on agriculture and commerce. Plymouth Pilgrims dug a canal to give them faster transport of produce to Boston. Pottery made in Salem in the 1640s was traded for iron made in Saugus and brass made in Lynn, or leather tanned in Plymouth. The coastal lands were not conducive to much more than simple sustenance. The settlers were not going to make it on crops. They had to be inventive, and they were, developing new, or improving on old-country ways to make shoes, clocks and watches, corduroy, paper.

Though freedom to practice religion had been the original impetus for coming here, rather than to acquire riches which is what sent explorers to South America, our early colonists were backed by British investors whose advances, plus interest, had to be repaid. The intrepid settlers were forced to develop into keen business people. And they did.

Once the debts were cleared, making money came to be an end in itself. Serious commerce began. Fleets of ships were built. Their holds had to be filled. In the earliest days they transported lumber and pelts to Europe and brought back products needed here. Then came the tragic triangle of fishery products and lumber traded for sugar, molasses, and rum—traded for gold and slaves. This created enormous wealth for founders of family fortunes, whose descendents refer to them simply as men of the sea.

Sailing ships built in Massachusetts ports opened America's China trade, a glorious story of high adventure and achievement, only somewhat dimmed by the tinge of opium. For the last quarter of the eighteenth century, Massachusetts ships carried over one-third of the entire nation's international commerce. During the same period almost 90 percent of America's fishing fleet was built and docked here. This included those ships used for whaling, which was an entire industry in itself.

*Hatch Memorial Shell, Charles River Esplanade*

While our fleets were among the world's finest and most financially successful, we were simultaneously expanding every kind of manufacturing facility. Gigantic paper mills, small cities of shoe factories, woolen and cotton mills were being built all across the state, many of them along waterways which provided sufficient and basically free power. The industrial revolution in America began when Francis Cabot Lowell put together in Waltham a factory that could for the first time, on looms he had perfected, complete all the operations for the manufacture of cloth under one roof. This was a considerable advance from the first filling mill built in Rowley in 1639.

During the nineteenth century, Massachusetts was producing 50 percent of the nation's output of boots and shoes, more than a third of its woolens, and most of its cotton textiles. Our dominance in cotton production came about because of machinery developed in Bridgewater in 1786.

It was this industrial fervor that brought immigrants flooding into the state from both Canada and Europe, as the need for manpower went way beyond what the wives and daughters of struggling farmers could provide. As cited above, each new group brought values that have over the years enriched and become part of the sturdy and ever-independent character of Massachusetts citizens.

The other great gift of that flamboyantly successful industrial period is a legacy of educational, literary and artistic, medical and scientific institutions, established and supported at least initially by the vast wealth that was generated—institutions which continue to provide Massachusetts a leadership role in those areas even to the close of the twentieth century, and into the foreseeable future.

Throughout its history, regardless of what the economic base might be—farming, fishing, commerce, shipping, manufacturing, and in recent years research, technology, and finance—the import of matters of the intellect has never been forgotten.

Boston's Public Latin School for Boys opened in 1635, and in 1636 the General Court gave permission for a college in Newtowne, later to become Cambridge, which was the beginning of Harvard. The first printing press in America came into being, also in Cambridge, in 1638. By 1640 there were thirty booksellers in Boston alone. In 1704 the first American newspaper, the *Boston News Letter,* was published.

In 1810 the Philharmonic Society became the first orchestra in New England. The Handel and Haydn Society, which continues to thrive, followed shortly thereafter in 1815, the same year that saw the founding of the prestigious *North American Review,* and the creation of a "Peace Society," the world's first.

The first high school for girls in the United States opened in Boston in 1825. And, in 1829, the Perkins Institution for the Blind was founded.

One of the first libraries in the nation to be supported by public subscription, the Boston Public Library opened in 1852. Early on, each Massachusetts city and town had, and continues to have, a public library, which may make the state unique in this respect. The Boston Athenaeum, a treasure trove library, opened in 1807, but was then and remains the province of members only.

As a *non sequitur,* I offer two items of useless information: The first man to go over Niagara's Horseshoe Falls in a rubber ball was a citizen of this state. In 1897, Boston opened America's first subway.

Now on to more serious matters.

*Boat-building is an Essex tradition*

Visitors to Massachusetts are first struck with its physical beauty, from whichever direction the approach is made. If from the west, the lush deep greens of forested hills, or in autumn those same hills blanketed in red and gold, please the eye. Coming in mid-state, from either north or south, one sees river valleys edged by ranked orchards or cropped fields, and still in a few spots, herds of grazing dairy cattle.

The North Shore has deep-water harbors filled with handsome boats, some of considerable size. Nantucket and Martha's Vineyard have highlands overlooking the sea, and lighthouse outposts. Cape Cod and the South Shore are gentler in profile, with quiet shallow coves, sandy spits, and thousands of acres of salt marsh and cranberry bogs.

The forces of nature have been good to Massachusetts, giving it glorious diversity with both jagged, cliff-edged coastline and miles-long stretches of sandy beach, scrubby pine forests in some places and grand hardwood stands in others, land that seems to only grow rocks, and acreage as abundantly fertile as that anywhere else.

And of course a climate that people joke about. "If you don't like our weather, wait a minute, it'll change." However, Massachusetts weather is more moderate in all respects than our neighbors'—north, south, and west—so we usually have summers that are not too hot, winters that are not too cold, and springs and falls that are fantastic.

Best of all, Massachusetts has water, water everywhere. Thousands of lakes, ponds, rivers, and streams punctuate the state's 8,257 square miles. Flying over the Commonwealth, the impression is vast forest from ocean to mountains and border to border, pierced by bodies of shimmering water—with cities, towns, and villages scattered about, and here and there bits of open space. It is difficult to think of the state being densely populated when you look down on it from above.

Because of those wooded areas and all that water, the Commonwealth has an abundance of wildlife. As its climate makes it a transition zone for vegetation, so it is for wildlife. Massachusetts residents are fanatic bird watchers, and they have many species to watch and worry over, not only those that live here year-round, but flocks stopping by on their seasonal flights north and south. One of the two major bird migration routes in America passes over southeastern Massachusetts.

The Massachusetts Audubon Society is a world force in the study and protection of birds, but is only one of many such active bird groups in the state. They are too numerous to name. Similarly, there is a multitude of nature conservancy organizations, each one vociferous and highly effective in its specific purpose.

Rachel Carson's red alert for the environment, *Silent Spring*, was written after she witnessed the sudden, and at the time unexplained, death of songbirds in the Duxbury garden of her friends, Stuart and Olga Huckins. Citizens of that same community continue to sound environmental alerts decades later, the most recent having to do with a nearby atomic power plant.

While no Massachusetts town or city has not had acres filled or leveled and then covered with housing developments and/or business and industrial parks which once had been open or wooded, or in some cases considered wetlands, it is the rare town that does not have forces fighting to preserve those spaces that do remain open. The battle involves all levels of government—a battle lost as often as it is won—

*Provincetown houses*

but a struggle that has helped retain much of the landscape which visitors find so appealing, and residents hold so precious.

Seldom, I suspect, do the forces on either side of the development controversy recall that the revered Charles Bulfinch was in truth a developer as well as an architect. Part of the group that built for speculation grand Mount Vernon Street houses on Beacon Hill, Bulfinch, in fact, lost so much money developing projects that he eventually spent time in a debtor's cell. Nor, probably, do the opposing forces consider Boston's Back Bay, especially Beacon and Marlborough streets or Commonwealth Avenue, three of the city's prides, as the product of developers from an earlier period. We might wish the work of twentieth-century developers would age as well.

There are hundreds of natural areas in Massachusetts set aside as parks, land trusts, conservation land, public gardens, what have you. From the awesome Cape Cod National Seashore that preserves the high dunes at Truro, to Martha's Vineyard's white chalk Gay Head Cliffs rising above the surf as America's first registered Natural Landmark, to equally magnificent reservations all across the state are national, state, and local parks.

Then there are tiny pockets of green maintained by rural and historical societies or other private organizations. And, of course, formal designs in several cities, such as the Public Garden in Boston, immediately adjacent to the rougher but historic Boston Common.

It was on the pond in the Public Garden that Robert McCloskey's duck family in *Make Way for Ducklings* settled. Bronze replicas of that family now march along the path just inside the Beacon Street gate, and a duplicate set thrills children in a Moscow park, a gift brought about by Barbara Bush after she and Raisa Gorbachev visited Boston together.

The Quabbin Reservoir is the largest man-made water supply system in the world. Thirty-nine square miles of water are surrounded by 120 square miles of wilderness. Bumpus Park in Duxbury is less than a quarter of an acre, all that remains of the earthen pier from which fleets of King Caesar's globe-girdling sailing ships embarked in the nineteenth century. These very different pieces of land are cherished and used by residents and visitors alike. No one has to go very far in Massachusetts to find a quiet place to walk, to fish or swim or sail, to hunt or paint or take photographs, to just sit and think about the natural world. This is one of its most endearing qualities.

The Commonwealth's reputation for its man-made beauty, its superb buildings, both domestic and public, is well deserved and has for many years attracted architects from around the world. Thus Breuer and Gropius, Aalto and Saarinen, LeCorbusier and Pei followed Americans Henry Richardson, Frank Lloyd Wright, Ralph Adams Cram, whose time came after that of Bulfinch, Asher Benjamin, Solomon Willard, Peter Banner, Samuel McIntyre and other early American architects. Each created buildings that marked their period and further enhanced the already high quality of Massachusetts' architectural heritage.

This treasure is another of the Commonwealth's great visual assets, an aspect that gives the resident or visiting viewer pause, that can stimulate one's intelligence and imagination, can draw upon the emotions so there is a sense one's soul is soaring.

*An ornamental fountain in Stockbridge*

While the cities and the campuses are impressive for their modern buildings, these being the places where most of the modern architects worked, we generally first become aware of an abundance of splendid architecture in small towns and villages where handsomely proportioned houses from earlier periods surround well-kept greens that may also site at least one steepled white clapboard church, perhaps a columned courthouse, and frequently a bandstand or monument to war dead.

Many of these houses are true colonials, federals, or Greek revival, with a sprinkling of fine Victorians, Queen Annes, Italianate, and examples of other periods. Though everyone thinks of a shingled "Cape Cod" or a square white clapboard house with a center chimney as typically New England, in Massachusetts, as elsewhere, there are many different types of dwellings, from grand manors and elaborate row houses to streets of simple structures built for factory or mill workers. These simple structures have acquired dignity with age, and are eagerly acquired by the young and affluent.

Throughout, it is integrity of design and careful maintenance over many years that is remarkable. Many houses have been kept in order through generations of inhabitants, changing only slightly to accommodate conveniences such as electricity, running water, and central heating. Those that fell into disrepair have been restored. Now that antiques, as they are called, have become status symbols, one has to be careful not to ask the owner of an old house when it was "restored"—especially if that owner is proud of the fact that the house never needed restoration, so is considered "original."

Some historians attribute the number and quality of original Massachusetts buildings to economic conditions. In coastal towns, sea captains built great houses that became boarding houses when going to sea stopped paying well. As the captain's sons went elsewhere to seek fortunes, unmarried daughters stayed on in the family home. With limited income they could not remodel or modernize. They made do. Thus the many-paned, old-fashioned windows—some with bubbled or wrinkled, tinted glass— were not replaced with large panes when sheets of clear, machine-made glass became available, and wide pine floorboards stayed in place even when narrow hardwood flooring came into vogue. Who would know what a premium would be placed eventually on those old things that people could not afford to replace when new ways to house came along?

Thus, there are streets in many Massachusetts towns with houses bearing dateboards going back to the 1600s, many more with the 1700s and 1800s. Historical societies give out these dateboards after much research verifies the history of a building. Dateboards are looked upon as an indication of authenticity: the earlier the house, the more the owners want that public recognition. As we move toward the twenty-first century, early twentieth-century houses will be dateboarded and prized. History does not stop.

It is understandable that Massachusetts should be so conscious of architecture. Charles Bulfinch is considered America's first native-born professional architect—if we think of Thomas Jefferson as a genius who designed buildings as a sideline, only one of his many disciplines. Actually, Jefferson wrote letters of introduction for Bulfinch when the Boston native went to Europe to see its architectural "wonders."

Bulfinch was untrained except for keen observation. Yet his sense of proportion, his feel for design that would produce understated elegance, combined with his ability

*A classic Federal-era beauty.*

to plot construction using a variety of materials gave us structures that remain today prized parts of the nation's heritage. A Bulfinch work is a particular American classic.

Several of his houses continue to be inhabited in Boston and elsewhere. Among his commercial structures, Faneuil Hall, built and then rebuilt by him after a fire, is the most important stop on Boston's Freedom Trail. And, crowning Beacon Hill, in what was John Hancock's pasture, is the Bulfinch "New" State House, a building that became the model and set the standard for state houses throughout America.

Other standards were set by utilitarian but majestic mills constructed along the state's rivers, and churches built first of wood with white steeples reaching toward the sky, and then of brick and granite. Many universities took their architectural cue from Harvard's early buildings. And the "Cape Cod" label has been attached to houses all over the world that have nothing to do with the originals other than a simple roofline and basic symmetry.

Admirers of Henry Hobson Richardson come from everywhere to see a cluster of five buildings in North Easton that he designed for the Ames family. Oliver Ames made his money supplying shovels to the Union Army during the Civil War. He spent much of it creating the now-famous enclave of Richardson buildings which were landscaped by Frederick Law Olmstead to show off the work of leading sculptors and other artisans of that conspicuous period. Trinity Church in Boston remains one of Richardson's considered masterpieces.

In Springfield there are in two districts several hundred huge houses built during the high Victorian period by new manufacturing money. They, too, attract architects and historians, both for their quality and their condition.

There are thousands of bad buildings in Massachusetts, ugly and shoddy, offering only basic domestic or commercial shelter, but with so many others worth looking at, our eyes can skip over the dreck. As with finding that quiet green spot where we can contemplate nature, finding a structure whose quality will raise our spirits just by looking at it is very easy in Massachusetts. I can say, as one who came here and decided to stay, in the beginning it was because of what I saw. Both nature and civilization have been generous to Massachusetts.

It is impossible to pass with any regularity the site of an event significant, not just to Massachusetts but to the nation, without thinking for a bit, even if one does not pause, about being where recorded history occurred. The same thing happens when the site is tied to our cultural heritage.

There are dozens, even hundreds of such places in Boston: Old North Church, Kings Chapel, the Granary Burying Ground, the Old State House, the frigate USS *Constitution*, Bunker Hill, Paul Revere's house, to name only a few. Just crossing Boston Common can be an experience in looking back if one remembers all that happened over the centuries on or around those few acres in the heart of the city.

Across the river in Cambridge, back from the street, is the big yellow house where Washington lived and had his headquarters when he assumed command of the American Army—the same house in which Henry Wadsworth Longfellow lived years later and produced much of the poetry we all learned in school. Just down the street, the village smithy stood under a spreading chestnut tree.

*Silver-shingled, tidy Nantucket*

It is a common phenomenon for those who have studied British history or literature to remark upon their first visit to England, "It is all so familiar to me. I feel as if I've been here before." Familiarity with American history and literature produces the same feeling on a first visit to Massachusetts, because throughout the Commonwealth are reminders of our illustrious, or sometimes questionable, past.

In Lexington we see where decisive early battles of the Revolution were fought. Salem conjures witchcraft trials. In Quincy we view handsome houses that look much as they did when they were home to the Adams family. Consider the contributions of John and Abigail Quincy and later generations of that family. Dedham reminds us of Saccho and Vanzetti. In Duxbury, John and Priscilla Alden's house stands as authentic evidence of the stark existence those first settlers led.

At the other end of the state, in Deerfield, settled roughly half a century after Duxbury, you can walk along the street past grand houses and be amazed at their elegant, handsomely pedimented doorways and fine moldings inside and out. These houses were built when Deerfield was the western frontier. We can only wonder at the character of men and women struggling to make tillable land out of wilderness, while surviving—or in many cases not surviving—massacres from warring Indians, still taking pains to create dwellings that were aesthetically pleasing.

Farther west yet, and much later, were the Shakers. South of Pittsfield, straddling Route 20, lies the village they built at Hancock. Until the 1940s it was occupied by a few remaining, practicing members of the sect. Since then it has been preserved as a trust for its justifiably famous architecture and because it shows how these industrious, inventive people lived. After gaping at the round stone bar and the main residence with its sublime interior design, one's thoughts turn naturally to a philosophy that guided the daily lives of those who developed the gift to be simple.

No place in Massachusetts more richly combines the immediacy of history and cultural heritage than Concord. Here in this village to the west of Boston, Henry David Thoreau pondered nature and man's place in it. He also practiced civil disobedience by refusing to pay a poll tax. Ralph Waldo Emerson revived and espoused the philosophy of Transcendentalism. Louisa May Alcott wrote *Little Women* and most of her other books here, and Nathaniel Hawthorne began his serious work. Their houses are maintained today exactly as they were when these writers lived in them, so while wandering through old rooms filled with furniture that shows it was well used by active families, one might think some of them could walk in unexpectedly. Certainly the power of their presence is felt.

For many reasons, the most fascinating of these Concord relics is the Old Manse, not just because it was home to Hawthorne for several years and has several window panes on which he and his bride scrawled messages, but because it was also home to the Emerson family. Ralph Waldo Emerson wrote his first book, *Nature,* in the very room where seven years later Nathaniel wrote *Mosses from an Old Manse.* And it was from a window in this same room that an earlier generation of Emerson women and children watched the battle at North Bridge between local volunteers and British troops. A statue of a Minuteman stands now at the spot from which was fired the "shot heard round the world."

*June roses on Nantucket*

No one can follow the course of that battle through the still-open fields above the Concord River, with outlined cellar holes of farmhouses that were there and other clearly marked action sites, and not be humbled by the rough and basic beginnings of the United States, and at the same time admire the determined bravery of a handful of Massachusetts farmers.

Not known beyond a small circle of admirers, one of America's most brilliant women lived in the Old Manse. Sarah Alden Bradford Ripley (of the Plymouth/ Duxbury Aldens and Bradfords) was a self-taught woman in a time when it was considered necessary to educate only young men. She spoke and read Latin, Greek, French, German, and Italian, and was so learned in botany, mathematics, and philosophy that the president of Harvard said she could teach any and all of the courses his college offered. As a wife and mother, she also had domestic duties. To acquire quiet time so she might pursue her thoughts, she decreed that, in the best parlor, conversation would be conducted only in Latin or Greek.

She, Mary Moody Emerson, and Margaret Fuller, who lived in Boston but came frequently to Concord, joined with Bronson Alcott, Thoreau, Ralph Waldo Emerson, William Channing, and others to engage in discourse, with no notion that their thoughts would move beyond the distance of their own hearing, nor have any impact beyond stirring other intelligences. Standing in their rooms, surrounded by their books, one contemplates the silence and realizes that much of the ideal America has strived for was part of those Concord conversations.

Sixteen fifty, 1658, 1737, 1768, 1700, 1767, 1719. These are the dateboards on a row of houses on a street in Ipswich. Not a special street. Numerous Ipswich streets might have similar dateboards. These are not museums. They are houses in which people live, as people have lived in them since they were built. Most are within inches of the pavement. Streets were narrower then. (Though broadened to accommodate automobiles, these old Ipswich streets remain exceedingly narrow by current standards.)

Many houses tilt forward as if eager to greet you. Someone seeing them for the first time might think they are in danger of collapsing, but they have been leaning for centuries. They look comfortable, not ramshackle. Some have heavy plank front doors studded with large-headed nails which form a pattern. Iron nails were expensive. If the builder could afford them, he wanted everybody to know how well off he was, so he put them where they would be seen—in his front door.

Off the narrow streets, little lanes curve around behind or up hills. The lanes lead nowhere, but they contain more lovely old houses—1668, 1702—tucked in close together so they almost touch. In any open space that remains, there are patch gardens filled with scads of flowers growing tall in an attempt to reach the sun.

While no one famous lived in most of these houses, nor does now, walking or driving past them—houses that have been lived in continuously for 300-350 years,not only in Ipswich and Deerfield, but in many other Massachusetts villages—makes a powerful impression. Going back long before the Revolution, their generations of occupants span the nation's entire history. They were lived in while everything else was happening in America, no matter what, no matter where. Wars were fought here

*Snow-sculpted sands near Provincetown*

and abroad, won and lost. Discoveries were made. We learned how to fly and to go to the moon. George Washington was president, and George Bush. And still these houses stand, are being lived in, and will continue to be. The steadfast endurance of these simple structures that have sheltered centuries of lives can, when considered, lead to deep reverie, to an examination of perspective, perhaps even of priorities.

If your bent is literary rather than historical, consider the following as only an abbreviated list of major American writers, beyond those already mentioned in this essay, who are or were Massachusetts born, bred, or based:

Louis Agassiz, Conrad Aiken, Cleveland Amory, Anne Bernays, John Berryman, Henry Beston, Anne Bradstreet, Thornton Burgess, John Cheever, Lydia Maria Child, Emily Dickinson, Andre Dubus, T. S. Eliot, Robert Finch, Benjamin Franklin, Robert Frost, John Kenneth Galbraith, William Lloyd Garrison, Ruth Gordon, Edward Everett Hale, Elizabeth Hardwick, John Hay, Lillian Hellman, Nat Hentoff, Oliver Wendell Holmes, Julia Ward Howe, Mark A. DeWolfe Howe, William Dean Howells, the Jameses—Alice, Henry, and William—Sarah Orne Jewett, Justin Kaplian, Jack Kerouac, Maxine Kumin, the Lowells—Amy, James Russell, and Robert—Archibald MacLeish, Malcolm X, John Marquand, David McCord, Herman Melville, Samuel Eliot Morison, Edwin O'Connor, Mary Oliver, Eugene O'Neill, Robert Parker, Francis Parkman, Edgar Allan Poe, Sylvia Plath, George Santayana, May Sarton, Anne Sexton, Jean Stafford, John Updike, Dan Wakefield, Edith Wharton, John Greenleaf Whittier, Richard Wilbur, Edmund Wilson, Daniel Yergin, Jane Yolen—and we could go on filling in the gaps.

The work of these writers and so many more who have a claim on Massachusetts is an essential part of our living national culture. It is fascinating to inhabit a place where they did, or are doing, their writing; to be part of—if possible, or if it is not to consider and attempt to understand—the society that produced them and the environment from which they developed their thoughts.

While the presence of past writers is apparent in their work and frequently in the places they inhabited or wrote about, and the same might be said for living writers, the majority of current writers working here tends to keep a low profile. Yet the cities and the woods are full of them. Cambridge is the center of a large group of writers, those who are academic and those who write for the trade. During the summer both Martha's Vineyard and Nantucket cater to large numbers of famous-name writers, as well as persons well known for other reasons.

The Berkshires are popular for writers who wish a more sylvan setting. Meanwhile, all across Massachusetts, solitary writers—for after all writing is a solitary occupation—go about their work, producing books and other printed materials that people read or perform the world over, while at home they are regarded merely as that quiet little man who is only seen once a day coming out of the post office, or as that busy mother who always seems to be carpooling. When does she find time to write?

For writers, part of the Massachusetts allure is the plethora of great libraries in the state, public and academic, with their systems of inter-library loans so that almost any book that exists can be acquired. These libraries exist because of the extraordinary

*Just off the Mohawk Trail*

abundance of educational institutions in the state, from giants such as Harvard, MIT, Boston University, the University of Massachusetts, and Northeastern to Radcliffe, Wellesley, Smith, Amherst, Wheaton, Williams, Brandeis, Simmons, Emerson, Tufts, Hampshire, and literally dozens and dozens of others of all sizes and types.

Metropolitan Boston has one of America's densest student populations. Several hundred thousand young people (though students come in all ages) spread out across the cities and suburbs, giving the entire area a frenetic but highly stimulating atmosphere. They fill the streets, the public transportation systems, concert halls, markets— their mode of dress, whatever the style may be at the moment, adding texture to the sometimes *au courant,* sometimes dowdy fashions of ordinary citizens.

The Amherst, Holyoke, Hadley area—site of four major colleges and a university— is similarly crowded with students attending that consortium of schools, while in almost all other parts of the state, at least one institution of higher learning exists whether it be a community college, trade school, or Ivy Leaguer. Along with being one of the world's major medical and research centers, Massachusetts has to be considered a major center of private and public education from preparatory schools through the most advanced degree programs.

Because they live here, feel a sense of civic responsibility, and because highly educated people assume they might be better prepared than others to solve the public's problems, professional educators frequently become involved in city and state politics in Massachusetts. This always adds zest to an already volatile situation, but it does not always shed light.

Politics in Massachusetts has from the beginning been a battle for spoils. When Boston's long-time mayor, James Michael Curley, was known elsewhere for his time in a federal penitentiary, locally he was still regarded as Robin Hood. The poor loved him, while the rich had to laugh through clenched teeth at his wit, most often directed at them.

Anyone hoping to win elective office has to get down and dirty. The surface polish of Yankees is long-since gone, even though an occasional Yankee still gets elected. No group, beginning with the founders, has given up power without a fight. Saltonstalls and Lodges did not lose happily to Fitzgeralds and Kennedys. Minorities have to be majorities before they make much headway in elections. The occasional forays into the field of educators and other professionals merely gives the ferment another flavor, but seldom shifts for long the balances of political clout.

Massachusetts acquired the "Liberal" label because it alone went for Democrat candidates in a couple of national elections, and because many of the social advances made in the course of our history began in this state, the causes of liberal thinkers. But the state is also home to conservative thinkers of all grades and variations. The John Birch Society was founded in Belmont and is only one of many right-wing groups that flourish here.

Outsiders are more obsessed with "the L word" than are residents of the state, as outsiders are more obsessed with "the Kennedys," as if the family were a single entity. There are Kennedy supporters in the state, obviously, but there are also Kennedy haters. It is not residents of Massachusetts who clog the streets of Hyannisport trying to get a glimpse of the compound. No one here considers them America's royal family,

*Savoy Mountain State Park*

though there is considerable sympathy for the tragedies they have suffered, respect for what members of the family have contributed, and dismay at some of their actions.

There are other political names that bring Massachusetts residents to attention. The state was home to Presidents John Adams, John Quincy Adams, Calvin Coolidge, and John Kennedy. They represent a political spectrum that is typical of the state.

Two of America's top tourist attractions are in Massachusetts—Boston and Cape Cod. Cape Cod is many visitors' dream of a place to vacation, with its long sandy beaches, quaint cottages, good restaurants, summer theatre, deep-sea fishing, whale watching, and every kind of gift shop imaginable. It is all there. It exists, and every Memorial Day, if the merchants and others who cater to the tourists are lucky, thousands of people come and leave behind tons of money when they depart.

After they have gone, the real Cape resumes its everyday existence, which, though much more crowded now than it used to be, is not all that different from life in other small towns. Residents who have been invisible to the tourists (either because they actually went elsewhere during the season, or like the Portuguese in Provincetown, withdrew) reappear and go about their business. Labor Day is for these people another New Year's.

They are not colorful characters, and they don't live in cute cottages or speak in dialect. Their corner of the state is hard pressed to survive the onslaught of people upon whom much of their economy depends. It is a catch-22 situation, but one they endure because they would rather live on Cape Cod than any place else on earth.

People flock to Boston for different reasons, and Boston is prepared for them with sufficient visitor facilities of every sort. While it may not be the hub of the universe, it is the seat of a large portion of the nation's early history, and continues to be the best city on a human scale in which one can visit some of the world's finest museums, listen to a world-class orchestra plus many other extra-fine musical groups, see a smattering of professional drama and comedy, go to a major league baseball or basketball or hockey game, and do just about anything else one wants to do.

Boston's skyline has changed. Coming on to it from the sea either by plane or boat, it is no longer the golden dome of the State House or the pointed tower of the Custom House one sees first, but a twentieth-century metropolitan mix of contemporary skyscrapers rising out of clusters of eighteenth- and nineteenth-century brick and granite buildings. These high-rise structures might appear to be slightly embarrassed by their size, as exuberant teenagers can be embarrassed, but they are also proof of the old city's vitality.

Boston's 350 years have dealt kindly. While other cities outgrew themselves and seemed never to run out of money so that buildings considered passé were constantly being torn down and replaced by new, Boston had to gallantly carry on, making do with the old because there was no cash to raze and rebuild even if that was what was deemed best. Thus, the city retained its flavor, improving what was already there rather than replacing. It is this combination of old and new that visitors especially enjoy.

There was a period when "urban renewal" became the thing to do, and Boston raised money to do it. The buildings that disappeared then, even those on the

*Wellesley College*

"wrong side" of the Hill, to say nothing of Scollay Square and Boston's beloved Old Howard, a historic burlesque house, are mourned to this day. Boston's new city hall that arose in one of the cleared spots is either a magnificent example of contemporary architecture or a catastrophic monument to mediocrity, depending upon who is making the pronouncement.

It is this sort of discussion that leads to the conclusion that Massachusetts is a state of mind as much as a physical or political entity.

But the North End remains; much of the market has been gentrified but in ways that make it a kind of glorified village gathering place in the middle of a city. And the Back Bay retains its dignity, while stretches in Southie and other parts of the city are being rejuvenated. There is plenty in Boston to keep people happy as well as excite them.

And then, there are the Red Sox. It has been said that no other city supports its athletes with a vicious loyalty to match that of Bostonians—"Bostonians" meaning all those in the Commonwealth who root for the Sox, the Bruins, the Celtics, the Pats. While tailgate picnics may be the way to go at Harvard/Yale football games, brass knuckles and the Bronx cheer are the order of the day when fans defend their professional sportsmen, who unfortunately require frequent defending. Yet, as fervently as fans defend them, they also proclaim loudly, especially about the Sox, that they (meaning the team) will do whatever has to be done to lose a pennant.

When all is going well, when the Sox are winning, when the Bruins are on a streak, or the Celtics are cleaning up, a glow hovers over the entire state, a warmth of pride exuded by fans that is sufficient to melt glaciers.

Fortunately, Boston and Cape Cod are not all there is to see in the state. Nor do they have a corner on culture. At the far western end of the Commonwealth, in the beautiful Berkshires, there is Tanglewood, summer home of the Boston Symphony; and Jacob's Pillow, a living museum of dance in America; and a little bit north in Williamstown, there is the ultimate in summer theatre and the Sterling and Francine Art Institute with one of the finest collections of nineteenth-century French paintings anywhere. If you want natural wonders, try the only "natural bridge" in North America, near North Adams.

The best part of the Berkshires are the little hill towns that remain relatively undiscovered so that it is possible to drive leisurely up and down their roads, stopping to gaze across distant vistas or at tucked-away, picturesque farms. Because some of these places look as if they had been plucked from a calendar and set down up-country, one can have trouble with reality.

I was excited when I came upon a true country store in Worthington, one that still has the local post office, carries everything a body might need from pork chops to aspirin and homemade bread and has a coffee pot in the back. I told a friend, "It's no tourist trap. There's no scented candles." My friend went to see, then called to say, "First thing I saw when I went in, just to your right, a display of scented candles." So be it.

Coming east there is another natural phenomenon in Shelburne Falls—potholes that were created by glacial action eons ago, long before the Pilgrims, even before the Indians who gave the Mohawk Trail its name. Once a footpath, it is now a favorite trek for foliage fanciers every autumn.

*The Kennedy Library, Dorchester*

In the central part of the state, Old Sturbridge Village has been created by bringing early nineteenth-century buildings from other sites to simulate a working community of that period. It tries to do the same thing Plimouth Plantation does in its reconstructed 1627 village near where the Pilgrims landed. Both are highly educational as well as entertaining.

The houses along Hingham's Main Street—some call it the most beautiful Main Street in America—have always been right where they are. As has the Elmwood Post Office in Bridgewater. Commissioned by Abraham Lincoln, it is still functioning. Gloucester, the oldest seaport in the United States, is not as important as it once was to the fishing industry, but its fleet still plies the waters of the Grand Banks.

Something could be written about every town in the Commonwealth, which would make it easy to see why Massachusetts fascinates—the Sedgewick Pie in Stockbridge; Salem's Peabody, the oldest continuously operating museum in America; or America's only Sanitary Plumbing Museum. That one came into being in 1988 in Worcester.

Then there are facts: Crane & Co. in Pittsfield is the sole provider of paper to the U.S. government for the printing of money. The longest-running carillon concert series (1924-present) is in Cohasset. The motorcycle was invented in Springfield in 1901. Tom Thumb lived in Middleborough.

And more Massachusetts people who did things, women this time: Maria Mitchell, astronomer; Clara Barton, founder of the American Red Cross; Elizabeth Palmer Peabody, founder of the first kindergarten in the nation; Francis Perkins, first woman cabinet member; Lydia Pinkham, of Elixer fame; Mary Baker Eddy, founder of the Christian Science Church; Phyllis Wheatley, first black poet in America.

We must not forget the world's worst drivers. I have a theory about that. I don't argue the reputation is justified, but I think it is because Massachusetts, as a home of liberty and independence for all, imbues its citizens with certain inalienable rights. We do not like to be told we have to do something, or we cannot do something else. We are the only state in which drivers believe seat belts should be fastened when the car is in motion, but successfully recalled a law mandating just that because we would not be told we must fasten them. It is a primal instinct to resist doing what one is told to do—even if it may save one's life. Having to pay the highest automobile insurance rates in the country is part of the price for stubbornness.

I have heard Massachusetts called Taxachusetts, and there is considerable truth in that, though there are those who have moved out of state to escape taxes and been surprised to find they paid more in their new place of abode. Massachusetts is right upfront with its taxes, as it is with political payoffs and other unpleasant aspects of life. It goes back to basic truth again.

I did not intend to stay when I came to study; I just couldn't drag myself away. I have complained bitterly about all the things Massachusetts residents complain about, but I have also become very proud to be part of the ongoing history of this place. The pot is ever aboil. While the Commonwealth has its ups and downs economically—going from boom to bust and back again with some regularity—and politically more often losing its electoral votes than using them, there is always ferment. Massachusetts continues to be a state of firsts, building on a long history of marching to its own tune. It is a fascinating, stimulating, quite beautiful place in which to be.

A Civil War memorial in the city of Lowell. ◄ ◄ Now a part of the Salem National Maritime Historic Site, this 1762 mansion was built by Elias Hasket Derby. A Salem merchant who pioneered a new sailing route around Africa's Cape of Good Hope, "King Derby" is said to be America's first millionaire. ◄ Rockport, an old quarrying and fishing village on Cape Ann, is the North Shore's resort town, filled with shops, restaurants, and inns, all blessedly quiet during the "off-season." ▲

Gloucester's Wingaersheek Beach
is favored by families with small children. Its smooth rocks make
great climbing, and one can wade out forever in calm, warmish
water. ▲ Plum Island is a world's-end kind of place—a long barrier
beach, most of it in the Parker River National Wildlife Refuge—more
than four thousand acres of dunes, bog, tidal marsh, and sand. ▶

In the 1830s, the entire brick mill city of Lowell suddenly appeared astride Pawtucket Falls, a thirty-foot drop in the Merrimack River. Built as a cotton textile factory in 1837, the Boott Mill is now a museum in Lowell National Historical Park, dramatizing the story of America's first major, planned industrial city. ◄ Lobstering is a more than $40-million annual business in the Bay State, and it is growing. A record sixteen million pounds were landed in 1990. ▲ Men of Newburyport and Gloucester continue to fish along the George's banks as they have since colonial times. ► ►

Scituate is an old town which has almost become a Boston South Shore suburb, but not quite. Nineteenth-century summer cottages still line the shore, and one can still learn to sail here, and rent what you need to fish. ▲ Springdell Farm in Littleton has sold pumpkins from its Route 119 farm stand since 1931. As the number of Boston area farms dwindles, the survivors are treasured for both their fields and produce. ▶ Cape Cod's beauty combines wind-washed vistas and very small, delicate details, like unexpected pink petals in beach grass. ▶ ▶

The *Mayflower II* is a brightly painted little tub of a ship. Still her message is jarring. Imagine squeezing into her prototype, along with 127 others bound for an uncertain voyage across the Atlantic. The replica is owned and operated by nearby Plimoth Plantation, a museum village dramatizing life in "America's Home Town"—in the 1620s. ◄ Hydrangeas are among the many flowers banking Nantucket's shingled houses. ▲

Boston's North Shore tacks and jibes around Cape Ann, along the ragged edge of Ipswich Bay and on to Newburyport. It is faced primarily in invitingly smooth rocks but also harbors myriad beaches. Many, like this Manchester strand, are private, but less so in the winter when walkers are welcome. ▲ A Dutch settler from New Amsterdam visits Plimoth Plantation, an annual October reenactment which coincides with three days of feasting and sports—the original Thanksgiving. ▶

In 1621, the Wampanoag Indian Chief Massasoit welcomed the Pilgrims to Plymouth, encouraging his tribesmen to help the newcomers farm, fish, and hunt. His statue now stands atop Coles Hill, near the sarcophagus containing Pilgrim remains. ◄ Judge Isaac Winslow built his handsome Marshfield house in 1699. It was remodeled in 1750 and served as a tearoom in the 1920s, but still retains its original staircase and hearths, some Pilgrim furnishings, and even a secret space for hiding Tories. ▲ Saltmarshes, like these along the North River in Norwell, were prized by the early settlers for their salt hay. ► ►

The smooth waters of Cape Cod Bay invite walking and shelling. ▲ Houses framed in flowers crowd along Provincetown's two narrow streets. This easternmost town in America has always been an escape hatch. The sober Pilgrims left it for rowdy fishermen and privateers to settle, and it continues to draw a lively mix of residents and visitors. ► Cape Cod is a seventy-mile arm of land thrust out to sea, fringed with sand, most of it public. So there's plenty to go 'round, especially on the "Outer Cape." ► ►

$G$reat Beach, preserved in its entirety as part of Cape Cod National Seashore, stretches thirty-nine miles along the open Atlantic, from Cape Cod's elbow to its outer tip. ◄ Carver boasts more cranberry bogs than any other town in Massachusetts. In October billions of red berries bob on the surface of bogs along Route 58 and Federal Furnace Road (Cranberry Alley) in South Carver. ▲ Sand fences discourage dune walking, and encourage dune grass to thatch the sands against erosion. ► ►

$S$agamore Bridge is the northernmost of two two-lane highway "hinges," which link Cape Cod to the rest of Massachusetts. A notorious bottleneck on Friday and Sunday evenings during the summer, the Sagamore is fondly viewed as the gateway to summer by generations of Bostonians. ▲ Summer cottages line the long ribbon of beach along Route 6A in North Truro, the thin wrist at the end of Cape Cod's "arm." ▶

A special light washes over the narrow, sand-rimmed stretch of the outer Cape that is North Truro. Generations of artists have gathered here to paint the play of sun and shadow on summer cottages against an expanse of sky. ◄ Buzzards Bay Railroad Bridge was a 1930s engineering marvel: its single-track span usually rests 135 feet above Cape Cod Canal. It is lowered in less than two minutes for freight and passenger trains. ▲

B‌lue Hydrangeas are indigenous to Cape Cod's iron-rich soil. ▲ The only Cape Cod windmill still on its working site stands by Route 6 in Eastham. Said to be built in the 1680s in Plymouth and subsequently moved to Truro, then to the nearby salt pond before finally settling here, the landmark continues to grind meal. ▶ Plymouth, "America's hometown," is home port for more than seventy-five lobster and fishing boats. ▶ ▶

Motels and cottages line the bluffs high above quiet beaches along Cape Cod Bay. ◄ Low tide and sunset in Provincetown, a time to stroll and fish. ▲ It is said that initial attempts to erect a lighthouse at Nauset Beach in Orleans "found obstinate resistance . . . as it would injure the wrecking business." The present Nauset Light is visible from seventeen miles at sea. ► ►

At the entrance to Peter's on the Canal, the Episcopal church in Bourne, parishioners are reminded of the Cape's link with the sea. Bourne is the home of Massachusetts Maritime Academy. ◄ Summer houses line beachside Commercial Street in Provincetown East End. If you don't happen to own one of your own, you will have little problem finding a "guesthouse," a breed of lodging that has been replaced by B&Bs and inns elsewhere in New England. But Provincetown has always marched to a different drummer. When in Provincetown, a guesthouse is the place to stay. ▲ Just one more spectacular Provincetown sunset. ► ►

As Cape Cod narrows, its beauty condenses. The leafy shade of Cape Cod National Seashore's Atlantic White Cedar Swamp Trail in Welfleet lies within earshot of surf pounding on the beach at Marconi Station. Trail markers note a surprising variety of plantlife in little more than a mile, the nuances of seashore life. ▲ Primitive cottages in the Provincetown dunes predate the Cape Cod National Seashore. Ultimately doomed, they are presently prized by P'town's artistic and literary community. ▶

The twenty-seven-thousand-acre Cape Cod National Seashore, established in 1961, preserves much of the Outer Cape's forest, heath, and sand. It monitors activities such as dune buggy riding in the Province Lands near Provincetown and the natural changes as winds and water sculpt and re-sculpt sand. ◄ "A man may stand there and put all America behind him," Henry David Thoreau commented in the 1850s, about the beach near Race Point—words to be savored with a Provincetown sunset. ▲

Pilgrim Lake in Truro reflects the sky between the Parabolic Dunes and the narrow strip of land, just wide enough for Routes 6 and 6A at Beach Point in North Truro. ▲ Provincetown is a two-mile, two-street-deep town along a beach-lined harbor. Its year-round population of four thousand swells to fifty thousand in summer. ▶ Walking the flats along Cape Cod Bay. ▶ ▶

In 1859 a Providence man had a small cottage—its eaves dripping fanciful wooden carvings—shipped over to Martha's Vineyard to house his family during the annual Methodist camp meeting. Similar confections with which his summer neighbors quickly replaced their summer tents still circle the open-air Tabernacle in Oak Bluffs. ◄ New Bedford seamen may hunt small scallops now instead of mighty whales, but their more than three hundred scallopers and draggers still add up to America's most lucrative fishing fleet—blessed anew each year in mid-August. ▲ Fog rolls in along the beach in Marshfield. ► ►

G ayhead Cliffs, a clay wall soaring 150 feet above the sea, is said to contain fossils of camels, whales, and wild horses. Its sunset colors also draw tourists to this southwestern tip of Martha's Vineyard, home of the Gayhead Indians. ▲ Less elegant than Edgartown but livelier than Vineyard Haven, Oak Bluffs is the summer boating and puttering-around center of Martha's Vineyard. ► Nantucket is half the size of Martha's Vineyard, takes twice as long to get to, and still wears its eighteenth-century Quaker uniform, sheathing its houses in modest grey shingle. ► ►

Springfield vies with Worcester for the title of the state's "second city." Its best-known site is the Basketball Hall of Fame which tells how Dr. James Nasmith first threw a soccer ball into a peach basket in 1891. It also profiles hundreds of basketball greats throughout the game's history. ◄ More than forty authentic buildings have been gathered from all over New England to form Old Sturbridge Village. Based on research, the museum village recreates daily life in an early nineteenth-century New England community—its farms, homes, shops, and grist mill. ▲

Colonel Ephriam Williams, Jr., wrote a will in 1755, giving West Hoosuck a "free school forever," provided the township fall within Massachusetts (instead of New York) and be named Williamstown. Williams died fighting the Frenchmen and the Indians, and the conditions of his will were eventually met. Williams continues to rank among the country's top colleges. ▲ At 3,491 feet, Mount Greylock is the state's highest peak, dominating North Berkshire. Its crowning ninety-foot granite memorial is dedicated to all Massachusetts men killed in war. ►

Students at the Quinsigamond Community College in Worcester take advantage of sun and snow. ◄ Tanglewood's Music Shed in Lenox is the cultural heart of the Berkshires. The fan-shaped, open-sided concert hall, the site of the Boston Symphony Orchestra's June through August concerts, holds six thousand, less than the number of music lovers who usually gather on surrounding grass during a weekend concert. ▲

The Worthington Corners general store is the gossip and commercial center of one of the classic old New England villages forming the Hampshire Hilltowns which are scattered throughout the high, gently rolling country between the Connecticut River and the Berkshires. ▲ South Berkshire is one of the least-touristed, most rural corners of Massachusetts. ▶

Route 2 shadows an old Indian trail across Massachusetts. It is a highway from which branch a multitude of country roads, like so many veins on a leaf, leading to river and hill towns, to many of the most beautiful, least explored corners of the state. ◄ Fall is the time of year to stray down country roads for no better reason than seeing trees colored like torches. ▲ After the "peak" autumn colors come softer, faded hues and the bright light of late harvest near Sheffield in South Berkshire. ► ►

The "Miss Worcester" remains a popular haunt. In 1891, C. H. Palmer registered the first patent for a lunch wagon design, and the Worcester Lunch Car Company later minted diners for much of the country. ▲ Worcester claims to be New England's geographical heart. In the Common at its own heart, settlers' graves and a Civil War monument are dwarfed by Worcester Center, an office and shopping complex. ▶ Northampton is the dining and shopping center for the Five College Area of Western Massachusetts. The five colleges are Smith, Mount Holyoke, Amherst, Hampshire, and the University of Massachusetts. ▶ ▶

This house in Stockbridge long housed some five hundred paintings, drawings, and sketches by one of America's most beloved artists. Rockwell lived his last twenty-five years within walking distance of this house and used this street as the background for his quintessential Main Street. ◄ In the Five College area of Western Massachusetts, foliage colors are reason enough for an annual "Mountain Day." On some particularly clear and colorful October morning, college bells ring and students stream off on bikes and on foot, celebrating nature's annual gift. ▲

Hancock Shaker Village looks like a primitive painting: set against its own orchard and meadows, a scattering of tidy buildings around the 1830 Brick Dwelling. Founded circa 1790, this "City of Peace" prospered in the mid-nineteenth century with some 250 Brethren divided among six "families." It survived for 170 years. The guides, craftsmen, and furnishings all tell the story of these dancing monks and nuns who turned farming, craftsmanship, and invention into visible prayers. ▲ On Patriot's Day, Minutemen and British soldiers again assemble on Lexington's town green to reenact the events of April 19, 1775. ▶

A Charles River sculler slips quietly between green islands just beyond earshot of the traffic on Storrow Drive. ◄ The Boston Symphony Orchestra, one of the largest orchestral corporations in the world, is based in Symphony Hall, known for its exceptional acoustics and a classical setting. ▲ Approaching Boston from the air, one is struck by the compactness of this peninsula city, now bristling with glass and steel high rises, still the "hub" of pleasant, but less distinctive, urban sprawl. ► ►

The ultimate Boston stroll is along Commonwealth Avenue when the magnolias are blooming. ▲ The USS *Constitution* takes her annual Independence Day turn around Boston Harbor—to Castle Island and back to her berth in the Charlestown Navy Yard. ► The Boston Public Library in Copley Square is one of the oldest and grandest of the country's big city libraries, an Italian Renaissance-style public palace. ► ►

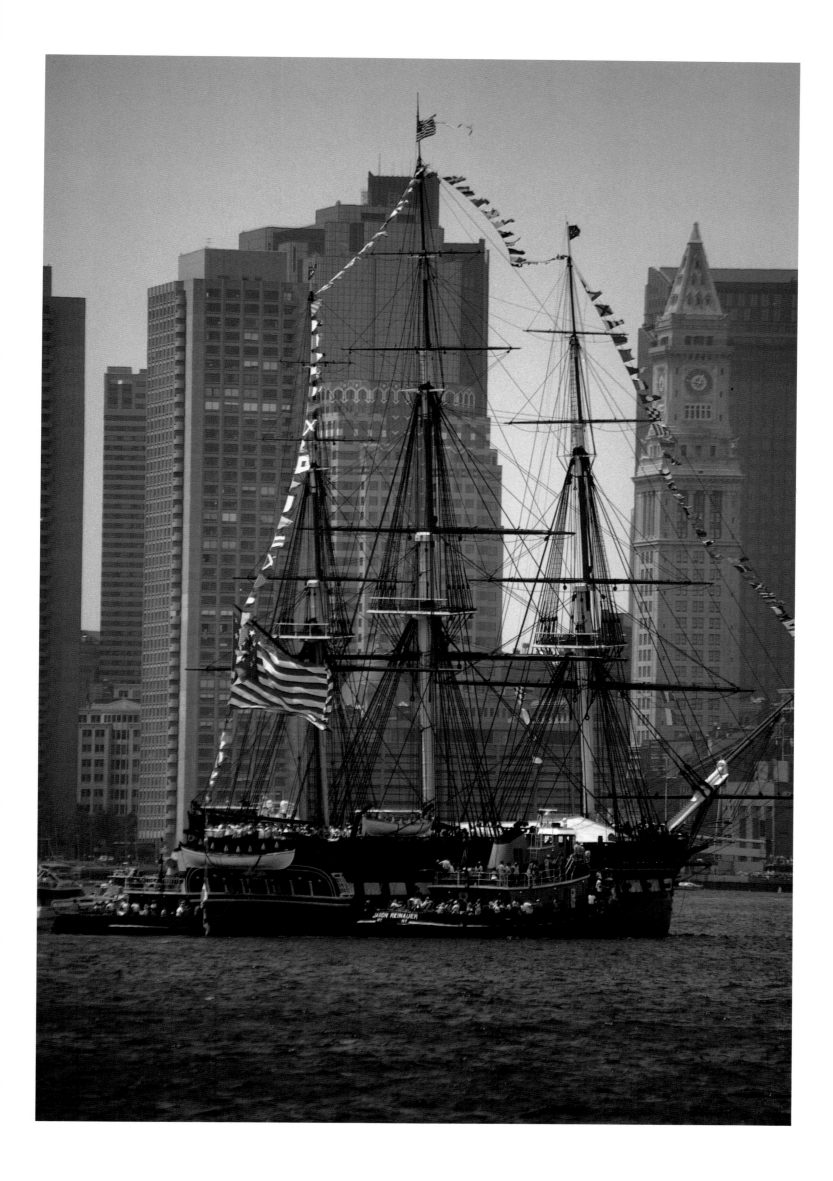

The gold dome of the State House, designed by Charles Bulfinch and first sheathed in copper by Paul Revere, crowns Beacon Hill, itself an urban jewel set between downtown Boston and the Charles River. ◄ Graduates of the Massachusetts Institute of Technology continue to affect the economy of the state (as well as the world) out of all proportion to their numbers. One in five MIT students joins high-tech companies in the immediate area, many founded by former alumni. ▲

$W$hat is said to be the world's shortest suspension bridge spans the ornamental pond in the Boston Public Garden. Its height is designed specifically for skaters to pass beneath. ▲ Some 130 Minutemen assembled on Lexington's green at 2 A.M. on April 19, 1775. Though they were not looking for trouble, they were not taking any nonsense either. It was almost dawn when their drummer sounded the alarm, and seventy men faced the British Regulars. It is still debated who fired first. ▶

Harvard University, situated in Cambridge, is the country's oldest and one of the world's most prestigious universities. Just 6,700 of its 18,300 students are under-graduates, but there is still a special pride to the college, whose graduates include six presidents. The ten graduate schools—most notable among them, law, medicine, and business—draw students from ninety-eight countries. The Weld Boat House is home for the women's sculling team. ◄ Luxurious student "houses" along the Charles River are known collectively as Harvard's "Gold Coast." ▲

The statue of John Fitzgerald Kennedy, thirty-fifth president of the United States, Boston born and educated, is ceremoniously unveiled at the Boston State House with a number of the "Kennedy clan," including Massachusetts Senator Edward M. Kennedy, in attendance. ▲ The legendary Larry Bird pits his skill against the New York Knickerbockers—who stand no chance on the Celtic's own home turf, Boston Garden. ▶

Boston is a peninsula city, a walkable space between a river and a harbor. Community Boating, just south of the Longfellow Bridge, encourages everyone to sail the river. ◄ Shellfish are among the many buys in the Boston Haymarket, a pushcart market held every Friday evening and all day Saturday at the city's commercial core. ▲ Fenway Park is one of the country's few surviving old-style, big-city baseball parks, still in the middle of the city and still small enough so that you can see the fans in the bleachers. It is real grass too, not plastic. ► ►

Saturday soccer games are a spring and fall ritual in the Boston suburbs. ▲ On Patriot's Day, Minutemen and British soldiers face off in Lexington before dawn. Later, they parade around Concord and reenact the 1775 skirmish at North Bridge, the "shot heard round the world." ► Year-round, Arnold Arboretum in Jamaica Plain draws Bostonians. The unusual park—its land given by the city of Boston, developed by Harvard University, and landscaped by Frederick Law Olmstead—displays approximately seven thousand different kinds of trees, shrubs, and vines from around the world, planted in family groupings. ► ►

$B$oston Common, the country's oldest public park, has marked the center of town since the 1630s. Where cows once grazed and militia trained, office workers now stroll past eighteenth-century graves, nineteenth-century statues, and the soaring Civil War monument. ◄ John A. Kelley, age 83, warms up before the ninety-fifth annual Boston Marathon. This was Kelley's sixtieth Boston Marathon, and he completed the entire 26-mile, 325-yard course. Boston's is the country's oldest marathon. ▲

From its 1839 beginnings as a Methodist seminary in Vermont, Boston University has grown to be the largest independent university in Massachusetts. Its twenty-eight thousand students are drawn from all states and 120 foreign countries. Famous graduates include Alexander Graham Bell (class of 1874) and Martin Luther King (1955). ▲ The brick core of the Massachusetts State House was designed by Charles Bulfinch, its cornerstone laid in 1795 by Samuel Adams and Paul Revere. ▶

John F. Kennedy's assassination in 1963 was one of the most unifying events in modern history. More than thirty million people from throughout the world contributed to the building of this harbor-side library in Dorchester, a memorial which architect I. M. Pei has designed to suggest both a stark lighthouse and a thrusting boat. Visitors are first submerged in the sights and sounds of the early sixties, then emerge into the airiness of a soaring glass pavilion, a combination of action (the exhibits) and reflection, which suggested to Pei the character of John Kennedy. ◄ Massachusetts remains the nation's symbol of "where it all began." ▲